DEPAR
Pocketbook
3rd edition

By Brin Best & Will Thomas

Cartoons:
Phil Hailstone

C000038685

Published by:

Teachers' Pocketbooks
Laurel House, Station Approach,
Alresford, Hampshire SO24 9JH, UK
Tel: +44 (0)1962 735573
Fax: +44 (0)1962 733637
email: sales@teacherspocketbooks.co.uk
Website: www.teacherspocketbooks.co.uk

Teachers' Pocketbooks is an imprint of
Management Pocketbooks Ltd.

With thanks to Brin Best for his help in
launching the series.

Previous edition ISBN 978 1 906610 44 9

This edition published 2014
ISBN 978 1 906610 67 8

E-book ISBN 978 1 908284 69 3

British Library Cataloguing-in-Publication
Data – A catalogue record for this book is
available from the British Library.

Design, typesetting and graphics by Efex Ltd.
Printed in UK.

Contents

How to use this pocketbook

This book is for heads of department and curriculum leaders working in schools and colleges. It will be of value to the newly appointed, to those already established in the role, and to those aspiring to such posts.

Heads of department carry out a critical role in the management of schools and learning. The Department for Education (DfE) has rightly championed the role and formalised the standards that those carrying it out should reach. The National College for Teaching and Leadership in its former incarnation as The National College for School Leadership proclaimed middle leaders 'the engine room of change'.

In recent years there has been an even sharper focus on middle leaders driving the quality of learning and teaching in classrooms. The use of data to raise questions about the performance of teachers and learners has been brought to the fore and middle leaders are expected to play an active part in coaching and mentoring colleagues to perform. This is coupled with a reduction in the average number of teaching years that professionals have under their belts before they take on leadership roles. Overall the demands on middle leaders are probably the highest they have ever been.

How to use this pocketbook

But how do you make sure that you and your department/curriculum area are playing a full part in transforming teaching and learning at your school? This book aims to give you the practical advice that will allow you to do this and thereby become an even more effective head of department.

A key message throughout this book about improving your management and leadership skills is the need to make time to **reflect** on what you do in order to improve. The current pressures in schools do not make this easy, but valuing reflective time is an important rung on the self and department improvement ladder.

As well as encouraging you to be reflective about your current practice, the book contains a wealth of tried and tested practical strategies and techniques that get results. The self-evaluation at the end of the book provides a structured path to improving your department.

How to use this pocketbook

Whether you are new to the leadership role or an established head of department, we hope that you will find fresh perspectives and approaches. The book is designed to help you view the issues in your department from different angles, challenge the norms and traditions and ask the question: just because it's always been done this way, is it the best way? There is nothing more certain than change, especially in the teaching profession. As attitudes towards education change, so we need to adjust the way we do things. The old becomes the new once more; the new becomes the old.

If you are a **new** head of department, be excited by what is possible and build a programme of personal development around innovation. Challenge established practice and create fresh perspectives – tread new ground. Your role has WAY more influence than you may think.

If you are an **established** head of department, remember that appropriate change keeps people fresh and vital. Things you tried in the past that didn't work so well may just be worth re-examination. Challenging received wisdom in your superiors is a part of your role, but it can be very hard to do. This book offers you tools to approach these kinds of challenges. The courage, of course, must come from you.

How to use this pocketbook

The need for optimism closely coupled with pragmatism
A head of department finds many twists and turns in the road to success. Staff absence, a low budget or a particularly troublesome student can stretch your physical, mental and spiritual resources to their limits and the expectations placed on middle leaders these days are stratospherically high.

Both authors have lived the middle leader role and thrived in it. We've also worked alongside thousands of leaders as coaches, trainers and mentors and assisted them to develop skills, attitudes, behaviours and beliefs that bring out the best in themselves and their teams. Everything in this book is tried and tested. However tough the challenge, there are always at least three secret choices. Will calls them 'The CIA':

C **Change it:** those things around you that you have the power to change, including your own thoughts

I **Influence it:** use your influencing skills to persuade others to do things differently, change policies, etc

A **Accept it:** accept what cannot be changed or influenced, and move on to C and I

Exceptional teachers have the **wisdom** to differentiate between these three choices.

How to use this pocketbook

There is no 'right' way to use this book, but we offer the following suggestions to help you get started and make the most of it.

Tips for using the book

- Think about and record the **current** position in your department before reading the relevant chapter. The self-evaluation tool at the back of the book can help you do this in a semi-quantitative way
- Plan to work through the book a **chapter** at a time, sharing your thoughts with another head of department at your school as you do so
- Work through topics in the book with a **coach/mentor**, focusing first on those that matter to you most
- **Share** the ideas in the book with others, including members of your team, to promote discussion

Finally, be **realistic** about what you can achieve in the timescale available to you. It will take many years to implement all the ideas in this book successfully, so identify your priorities first.

Introduction

Managing Your Department

 Effective Documentation

Maximising Student Achievement

Raising the Profile of Your Department

Self-evaluation

Further Information

Managing Your Department

The developing role of the head of department

The Responsibility Triangle is a neat way to look at your role as an academic leader and focus on your development.

As a middle leader your role is to accept the responsibility for improving learner progress. This involves being accountable to your senior leadership team, parents, governors, and the learners themselves, whilst balancing the challenge and the support that you offer your team and yourself. Too much challenge and/ or too little support and colleagues can fail to make progress. Likewise, too little emphasis on accountability can lead to mediocrity.

This book sets out to help you '**raise your game**', whether you are an established or newly appointed head of department.

The department within the whole school

Targets for subject performance have become more demanding in recent years, and all examination subjects make a key contribution to the school's success. Measures of exam and test performances and value-added scores have all increased accountability.

There is a **balance** to be struck between the needs of the department and those of the school as a whole. Factors that might need to be considered in decision-making at middle leadership level include:

- The impact on **learners**
- The impact on the **department/ phase/ area**
- The implications for **other** departments
- The likely impact on the **school** as a whole and the school improvement plan
- The **public** implications – what will be seen externally?
- The **hidden** implications – what will go unnoticed or surface later?

Leadership and management defined

There is a **distinction** between management and leadership:

- **Leadership** is about mission, direction and motivation. It is the expression of vision and the motivation of others to achieve that vision. Louis and Miles (1990) define it as, 'mission, direction and inspiration'
- **Management** is the expression of leadership; the mechanisms by which vision is achieved. It is the 'designing and carrying out of plans...and...getting things done' (Louis and Miles 1990)

Leadership is the 'what' and the 'why'.
Management is the 'how' and the 'when'.

There is an **interdependence** between leadership and management in effective departments. It can be tricky to distinguish pure leadership from pure management, as many activities within each area actually overlap.

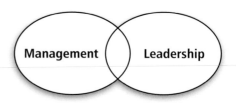

Models of leadership

In leading and managing, use a **process** for moving issues and teams forward.

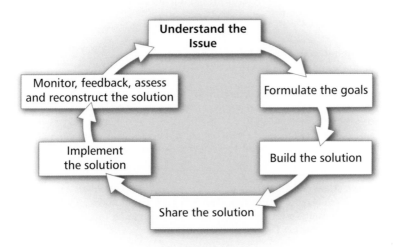

- Understand the Issue
- Formulate the goals
- Build the solution
- Share the solution
- Implement the solution
- Monitor, feedback, assess and reconstruct the solution

Vision in leadership

Vision is about **possibility**. A dream inspires people and galvanises them into action. When visions are shared and built up within a team they are powerful motivators. When teams all buy into the same dream amazing things can happen.

Begin with **generating** and **understanding** your departmental vision:

> *Vision today shapes your future tomorrow*

- **Developing** the vision and **communicating** it puts your future in the minds of those in your team. It raises your awareness and that of others and increases the network of people who know about it
- When plans are **exciting** and take people to new levels of thinking, people talk about them and opportunities to achieve them tend to be more noticed by the team and others

Developing a vision collaboratively with your team is a powerful way to bring them with you and raise the level of motivation. The four-step Vision-Builder Tool that follows is a tried and tested method for creating a powerfully engaging future representation of a team's outcomes. (Best & Thomas, 2008)

The Vision-Builder Tool

Step 1. The Visioning State. This involves preparing your team for the process. Explain why visions are important for teams and how they are meant to push at the boundaries of what we currently think might be possible. Therefore, the team should approach the process with a 'no limits' mindset. The question they can consider then is: *If there were no limits or constraints upon what we could achieve with our department, what would we want?* No idea is too far-fetched

Step 2. Generating Ideas. Give each member of the team a stack of blank sticky notes. Ask them to write only one idea on each note. Offer them these prompts for their ideas: *Imagine a future where everything is happening as you would like it in your classroom and this department in X years from now*.

- *What is happening in this new future?*
- *What are we seeing, hearing or feeling in this future?*
- *What is different now compared to back in (add current year)*

Keep writing until you run out of ideas.
(Note that questions and answers are expressed in the present tense to try to locate positive feelings in the here and now.)

The Vision-Builder Tool

Step 3. Defining the FUTURE. Lay out the notion of a timeline on the floor as it appears in the diagram on the next page but without the Control/ Influence/ No Control labels at this stage. Get the team to stand on NOW on the floor, and to walk out into the future and say and place their sticky note ideas into the FUTURE. If others share the same or similar ideas they can acknowledge this and place their ideas together in the FUTURE. Get everyone to share then go and stand in the FUTURE together. Ask them to feel what it's like now, imagining they already have this future. Let them 'feel' this future.

Next lay out the three labels of Control, Influence, and No Control. Ask your team to sort the future desires they have written down into three groups:

1. *We have control over this*
2. *We have influence over this*
3. *We have no control over this*

If you wish, you can also ask your team to prioritise those outcomes over which they have control or influence and begin to think about the timeline to achieve them.

The Vision-Builder Tool

Step 4. Embedding the Vision. With your team standing in the FUTURE position on the floor with their vision desires in front of them, get them to look back along the timeline into the past and ask them *what did we do to get here?* You are using past tense language to refer to a future which you are defining in the present tense. This kind of language shift unlocks more creativity and diminishes the impact of limiting thoughts on the process. Write down the responses on sticky notes and place them in order along the timeline. These steps become your action plan.

Control

Influence

No Control

Stand here on
NOW

FUTURE

The characteristics of winning leadership

Follow the model:

C is for:
- **C**hallenge – see roles/tasks as challenges not problems
- **C**reativity – engage creativity in meeting challenges
- **C**areful listening – listen to understand the issue before responding

P is for:
- **P**lanning – carry out planning in the long, medium and short term
- **P**urpose – have a clear sense about overall purpose of your role
- **P**riority – prioritise workload to meet goals

The characteristics of winning leadership

R is for:
- *R*esilience – take time out for mental, physical, spiritual and social renewal
- *R*eflection – take time out for you and your team to reflect on past events
- *R*eflexivity – pay attention to what you are doing, as you are doing it

S is for:
- *S*olutions-focused – believe that all challenges have solutions
- *S*trength-recognition:
    - know the strengths of the team and use them
    - know your own strengths and use them
    - give feedback recognising strengths
- *S*tay flexible – be open to new ideas and learning from whatever source

A useful way to recall these characteristics is through the mnemonic:
*C*areful *P*lanning *R*esults in *S*uccess

The characteristics of winning leadership

How do you currently rate your attitudes and behaviours?

The following activity will help you to look at your
leadership attitude:

1. Using the two previous pages, consider each of the leadership
   attributes in turn.

2. For each one, ask yourself the question: How consistently do I
   demonstrate this characteristic? Then score yourself out of
   ten, where ten represents excellence.

3. You may wish to get some feedback from others on this too.
   This can add objectivity.

4. From the results, pick an area you would like to develop
   further. Use the helping model on page 28 to guide yourself
   through the process of development in the chosen area.

Planning and goals

Fail to plan, plan to fail
Leslie Spears

One of the most critical aspects of the head of department's skill-set is **planning**.

Assess your current level of planning by asking yourself these questions:

How **confident** are you about your departmental goals for:
- Today?
- This week?
- This year?
- The next five years?

Rate your confidence using a scale of one to 10, where ten is 'completely confident'. Consider what you don't score, eg if you gave 8/10 what is the missing two telling you?

Goal setting

A goal is a dream with a deadline

Goals can help you achieve the success you want.

They:

- Are the key to **motivating** people
- Break vision into **realistic steps**
- Are the **what**, the **how** and the **when** of success
- Propel us towards **achievement** when properly devised
- Should be **reviewed** and **updated** periodically

Goal setting

When **setting** goals, focus on a number of important components:

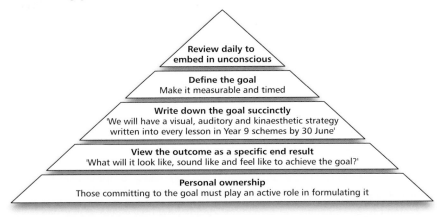

**Review daily to
embed in unconscious**

Define the goal
Make it measurable and timed

Write down the goal succinctly
'We will have a visual, auditory and kinaesthetic strategy
written into every lesson in Year 9 schemes by 30 June'

View the outcome as a specific end result
'What will it look like, sound like and feel like to achieve the goal?'

Personal ownership
Those committing to the goal must play an active role in formulating it

Ask yourself the question: **How realistic is it?** Review the details of outcome, timing and measurement according to the answer.

Creative thinking and innovation

Once you have formulated goals, next ask the question: **How do I meet these goals?**
Sometimes the question can be answered easily; at other times you may need a little
creativity.

Eight ways to think **creatively**:

1. **Generate** as many open questions as you can associated with the goal.
2. Allow **processing time** (permit your unconscious mind to consider the goal
   overnight or over a few days and embed it).
3. Use **bisociation** techniques (see next page).
4. Use **visual** techniques such as Logo Visual Thinking and mind-mapping.
5. **Share** the goal and the 'how' question with your team and get their minds
   working on it.
6. **Ask a layperson** (someone unconnected with your work) for some ideas.
7. **Search** the internet for a fixed time using key words from your goal.
8. **Pretend** to be someone you admire and decide how they would answer the
   'how' question.

Creative thinking and innovation

Bisociation techniques involve bringing together two ideas and are the brainchild of Arthur Koestler. They can be an effective way of finding a solution.

One way to do this is:

1. Give yourself time to relax and be away from distractions.

2. Take a sheet of paper.

3. Write the issue to be resolved in the centre.

4. Around it generate random words, ideas or pictures (you can ask others to help you).

5. Now consider each random idea alongside the key issue and see what it triggers in your mind.

6. Invite others into your bisociation process.

Creative thinking and innovation

Another successful technique for encouraging innovative thinking is to use **mind-mapping**:

- Choose a key word which represents your issue
- Write it in the centre of the page and draw a picture that represents it
- Draw lines from the central image
- Along the lines, write ideas as key words which come to your mind
- For each key word allow your mind to associate with it and draw further lines to write these on
- Draw images alongside keywords to further promote association

Benefits of mind-mapping:

- Encourages **associative thinking**
- Encourages **creativity**
- Enables **planning** at a detailed and overview level
- Makes choices clearer when **decision-making**
- **Summarises** large quantities of data
- **Improves recall** of large amounts of information

Mind Maps® were developed by Tony Buzan (see Buzan and Buzan 2000).

Creative thinking and innovation

Turning vision into action

With the vision broken down into goals and some creative solutions thought through, it's now time to commit the plan to paper in the form of an action or development plan. The example below outlines a suggested layout (note that it is for illustrative purposes only and does not give an exhaustive set of steps to achieve the stated vision). This plan will broadly outline the timing for the goals for the three years ahead.

Vision We have high quality display in every room and corridor around the dept. The display acts as a powerful and compelling medium for showing achievement, content and process in each year group				Contributors: MR, DC, TO, PA, BS, CA, SS, ST, BN
Goals	**Timing**	**Resources**	**Person responsible**	**Success criteria**
To decide the criteria for highly effective displays	Complete by 16 Oct	Time 1 hour – in dept. meetings on 19 Sep and 12 Oct	TO	A set of workable criteria for judging the effectiveness of displays
To identify the existing display areas and assess current quality with regard to appearance and function	Complete by 10 Nov	Time – book out period for PA, BS, SS to tour dept. and appraise resources	PA, BS, SS, with TO booking time out	A written assessment of the current quality of display, set against the criteria, is available

There are some questions on the next page which can help you check the accuracy of your action plan once complete.

Turning vision into action

Ten **questions** to ask yourself when turning your vision into action:

1. What exactly will it look, sound and feel like when the vision is achieved?
2. How will we know when we have achieved it?
3. How does this vision fit with our core values as a department?
4. What does the team think of this vision?
5. How motivated are we as a team to achieve the vision? Score out of ten.
6. What would make it more motivating?
7. What stands in the way of us achieving this vision?
8. What can we stop doing that would give us more time for this?
9. What are the steps involved in making this happen?
10. What will move us one step further forward to achieving this vision?

Turning vision into action

Once you have formulated your action plan and checked it meets your needs, you can begin to create the strategic plan for the coming year, half-term by half-term. Creating a term-long plan that lists week-by-week actions under themed headings might seem like a drag, but it is pivotal to keeping you on track.

Using sticky notes on large sheets of paper, or a software package, makes it easy to experiment and change. You can see each week's priorities at a glance, and even if you miss some of them, you won't let things slide because you know how the whole picture of change fits together. Your plan can also help you keep your team motivated towards your shared vision, allowing you to celebrate success each week. Include whole-school actions (eg report writing, consultation evenings, etc) on the plan, thereby keeping a realistic sense of workload each week.

Week	Assessment	Performance Management	Fundraising for charity	Curriculum replanning	Trips	Report-writing
1						
2						
3						

Turning vision into action

Once you have your action plan make it part of your **everyday** work and that of the department by:

- **Displaying** copies of the plan in staff meeting and circulation areas
- **Reviewing** progress regularly, eg in meetings and on weekly briefing sheets
- **Celebrating** the success as you move toward the vision
- **Referring** to your action plan every day and encouraging your colleagues to do the same*
- **Scheduling** the main dates in the plan – arrange a date with colleagues responsible for a section of the plan to meet up and discuss progress. Do this up to two weeks before the due date
- **Listening** carefully to issues arising in these meetings and using the creative solutions tools to overcome barriers to success

*Research on success points to the importance of writing goals down and referring to them every day, thereby embedding them subconsciously. This primes you to look for opportunities to achieve your goals amidst everyday tasks.

Building team spirit

Team spirit is the sense of **sharing values and goals** and working towards these goals in a positive and supportive environment. It is about members of a team feeling **valued** and each member feeling a sense of **belonging**.

What builds team spirit?

Come on, come on!

- **Shared** values and goals
- A genuine forum for **meaningful** expression of views
- Excellent **communication**
- A sense of **humour**
- Paying attention to the **professional** and **personal** needs of individuals
- **High standards** backed up with **celebration** of success
- Going the **extra mile** for your team
- Dealing **promptly** and **fairly** with personnel disputes
- **Empowering** staff to make their own decisions when appropriate
- Activities which **motivate** staff and promote a sense of belonging

Building team spirit

Fifteen ways to **build** and **maintain** team spirit:

- **Talk to your team** face-to-face as much as possible
- **Be around** at break/lunch to chat
- Have a weekly **briefing sheet** for the department
- **Be seen** around the department
- **Notice** good practice, displays, etc
- **Celebrate** what you see
- Start and finish meetings **on time**
- Ensure that **everyone** has an opportunity to say something when you meet
- Have **one-to-one meetings** with team members periodically, aside from appraisal – find out how things are going
- Arrange **social gatherings** in and out of school
- **Listen** more than you speak
- **Support** individuals in their professional development
- Provide opportunities for staff to express their **opinions** and contribute to **decisions**
- **Coach** colleagues by asking **open questions** to help them decide for themselves rather than telling them what to do
- Be **consistent** in your decision-making – use the core values of the department to make decisions

Developing rapport

Rapport is a relationship between two people which is filled with mutual understanding, trust, confidence and harmony. Rapport creates ideal conditions for exploring differences without conflict, and being able to establish effective rapport is a key leadership and management **skill**.

Rapport develops on a number of levels:

- **Physical** – our body language and eye contact
- Verbal **tone** – our tone of voice
- Verbal **language** – the words we choose to use

A number of researchers have tried to put figures to the proportion of communication that takes place at each level. All suggest that the **physical** and **tonal** aspects have more impact than the language. A key factor is making sure that all the levels are **congruent** – if your body language does not support what you are saying, this will be readily noticed by others.

Developing rapport

Develop better rapport through **learning style** preference.

People experience the world in different ways. Some more through what they see (a visual learning preference), some more through what they hear (an auditory learning preference), and some more through what they do and feel (a kinaesthetic learning preference).

You can notice the preference through the language a person uses, and respond using similar language:

- **Visual**: I see; it seems like a bright idea; that's clear to me

- **Auditory**: I hear what you are saying; that went with a bang; I will sound her out

- **Kinaesthetic**: I have a feel for that; I am in touch with this; I'm standing firm on this

Example of use: when responding to a staff member explaining a problem, show empathy by using words which match their preference.

Developing rapport

Develop better rapport through **pacing** and **leading**.

To build rapport you need first to **pace** the person. This means showing them **attention**. From here you can lead them towards rapport.

Mirror the other person's body movements subtly. Cross matching is very subtle, and involves matching the action of one body part with another, eg they cross their arms, you cross your legs. Consider:

- Mirroring facial expressions
- Matching or cross-matching limb movements
- Mirroring their eye contact
- Matching their body position

Once you have matched a person you can begin to lead them to new body language.

Example of use: this can be used effectively to build rapport in **meetings**. For example, where a colleague is negative, you can lead them physically towards the body posture of a positive person by leading them to sit upright, to smile, and to bring their shoulders back and to breathe more slowly and deeply.

Coaching

Coaching is another valuable skill worth developing. It refers to a way of working with people which empowers them to make changes in the way that they work. Coaches believe that we all hold the solutions to our challenges **within us**, and that we can work out how to resolve issues ourselves. Coaching:

- Is **non-judgemental** and **non-critical**
- Maintains the coachee in a **positive**, solutions-focused mindset
- Uses the skills of listening, questioning, reflecting and clarifying
- Encourages individuals to break **goals** into manageable **steps**
- Works through **open questioning** rather than **telling**
- Is concerned with **motivation**
- Helps individuals to overcome **self-limiting** thoughts and behaviours
- Leads individuals to commit to **change**

Example of use: when a colleague comes to you with a problem, ask them about the issue and listen. Then use the STRIDE model on page 38 to help them to create a solution that is tailored to their needs. This empowers them and frees you of the burden of thinking through their issue later.

Coaching

Coaching exists in a **variety** of forms. **Non-directive coaching** is one of the most powerful. Even if the end result of a coaching conversation is to achieve something required by the school, coaching can create choice and, therefore, motivation in others because it enables them to have ownership over the way they approach their work.

Coaching revolves around a **sequence** of questioning which is part of the so-called 'STRIDE' model:

Strengths – What's currently going well?
Target – What do you want to be different?
Reality – What's preventing you having this target?
Ideas – What are the possible ways you could move towards this target?
Decide – What will you definitely do as a result of this conversation?
Evaluate – (At a future point). How did you get on with the action you decided to take?

(For more information about STRIDE see *Coaching Solutions Resource Book* by Will Thomas, 2005).

Mentoring

Mentoring differs from coaching in that mentoring includes the offering of **advice** and **guidance**. Mentoring, like coaching, can have multiple styles, and to some extent coaching and mentoring overlap.

When mentoring staff, students or student teachers:

- Set high expectations and show you believe in their abilities
- Encourage self-reflection with questions
- Meet regularly and make sure the time is not interrupted
- Use a variety of learning approaches, eg discussion, resources, practice
- Believe that teaching is skilful and can be learned
- Plan the programme of mentoring carefully, yet be flexible
- Create opportunities for teachers to see others teach and reflect upon this
- Provide **balanced** feedback

Example of use: a newly qualified teacher is struggling to put across a difficult concept to his students. You have a set of steps which have worked well for you. You explain your approach and ask him how he might tackle the topic using these ideas.

Influencing skills

There are times when we need to **influence** others positively about a course of action. This might be a member of your own team, a student, a parent or a member of your senior leadership team:

- Be clear about how what you want **fits** your **values** and your **vision**
- Be clear what you want to **achieve** by this action and what the benefits are
- Consider the **consequences** of your action
- Predict likely **contrary views** and decide how you will manage them
- State clearly what you **want** and **feel**
- Listen **carefully** to what the other party **wants** and **feels**
- **Repeat back** to them what you have heard them say
- Repeat what **you** want/need
- If your needs are not met, **continue** to repeat again, calmly, your needs
- If you feel **intimidated**, take a trusted colleague as support – brief them first

Finally, it is important to accept that there will be times when you will **not** be happy with an action taken in your school. Do your best to put your opinion forward constructively, then move on – there is no point in holding grudges for things that happen against your wishes.

Influencing skills

When might you need to influence others?

Example 1: You are asking the headteacher for money for a special project. *Tip*: be clear about the benefits. Support the request with data. What data exists now about the problem? How is this data likely to change if the head agrees to your request?

Example 2: Your school timetabler asks you for the use of a member of your staff to teach in another subject next year. The teacher is currently suffering from stress. You are concerned. *Tip*: empathise with the timetabler. Try to see their point of view. Articulate your concerns. Engage positively in a search for alternatives or support, but be clear about the potential impact on the member of staff concerned.

Example 3: The head of sixth form urges you to take a student on to your A-level course. This student showed little motivation for the subject at GCSE and failed to achieve the entry requirements at GCSE to progress to the A-level. *Tip*: find out precisely why there is an insistence on the student returning. Ask the questions: what are the costs and benefits of the student doing the subject? How will we be serving this student if we allow them on to the course? What other solutions are there?

Seek a win/win solution wherever possible

Getting the best for your department

There will be occasions when you need to get the **best** for your department in the face of pressure. Balancing whole school and departmental needs can be tricky when you are confronted with an issue that requires immediate action.

Consider the following guidelines:
- Be clear about what you want to **achieve** from the discussion
- Know the **facts**: what is being requested? What are the costs/benefits?
- Emphasise what you can **agree** to
- Explain clearly the **consequences** of the action which is being proposed
- **Separate** the person from the issue - stay calm
- Ask for **time** if you need more information or thinking space
- Seek **alternative** solutions with the person making the request/demand
- Look for a **win/win** situation, but be prepared to stand up for your beliefs
- Finally, accept that a decision-making **hierarchy** exists in your school and you are **not** yet at the top of it!

Sometimes our emotions well up when requests are made. The first step in dealing with requests is to **Listen**, then to **Question**, then to **Analyse** and finally, to **Decide**.

Lesson observation

Regular **lesson observation** should be a feature of every department. It is important because it:

- Allows you to monitor the **quality** of teaching and learning in your subject area
- Can determine specific **training needs** for individual teachers
- Reveals **good practice** that can be shared with other members of the department
- Gets colleagues **used to** being observed, reducing anxiety when inspectors observe them

Encourage all the teachers in your department to observe each other as part of a rolling cycle and make sure **you are observed** too. Lesson observation is an extremely effective mechanism for improving departmental practice. It is now firmly established in schools as part of performance management.

Remember: few of us improve without feedback, and lesson observation is an excellent way to gain useful feedback about your teaching.

Lesson observation

The most effective approaches to lesson observation come from shared ownership of the process. 'Joint Evidencing' (JE), empowers both observer and observed.

Before the observation:
- Agree a specific focus
- Develop the criteria for success (or use those already available in school)
- Plan the timings for the observation and feedback

During the observation:
- The observer focuses on the criteria that are pre-agreed
- Evidence and timing of events which supports these criteria are noted down throughout

After the observation:
- Find quality time to review the observation very soon afterwards
- Conduct the review meeting on the basis of evidence that you and the person being observed saw, eg *'I saw evidence of this, but not this; did I miss something? What did you notice? What was your intention at this point?'*
- Keep the focus on evidence and away from judgments and points of view
- Agree action points and timescales for following up any areas for development

Giving feedback

Feedback is a vital tool for helping people to learn. Where it cannot be joint-evidence-based the following guidance can be helpful. Keep it:

- **Balanced** – with a ratio of four strengths to one developmental point
- **Specific** – state exactly what was good and what specifically could be improved, avoiding platitudes like, 'that was great'
- **Solution-focused** – 'You could make this even better by…' or a question… 'What would make this even better?'
- **Often and immediate** – happening along the way rather than all at the end
- **Genuine** – it needs to be delivered with congruence in word, tone of voice and body language: you have to mean it!

Managing meetings

All too frequently meetings are used as ways of passing information on and for administration rather than for furthering the **vision** and **success** of the department.

For effective meetings:

- Use other ways of communicating **information** – briefing sheets, memos
- Circulate an **agenda** in good time – give timings to each item
- **Start** the meeting on time and **end it** on time – don't be afraid to challenge lateness or people who overrun on their item
- Make the **first item** a fixed discussion, eg 'update of best practice in the subject'
- Limit time on **administration** to say 20% of meeting time – it expands to exceed the time you give it!
- Make meetings **productive** in terms of attention and outcome by exploring ideas with your team – encourage discussion
- Plan key items for discussion in **advance** throughout the year – and communicate these early
- Encourage **others** to lead items, freeing you to manage the meeting

Performance management

It is your role to support the development of your team towards excellence and one of the key tools to enable you to do this is the performance management framework (PM).

Schools and colleges have their own approaches to performance management and ways of linking it to performance-related pay. There are some basic principles which can help:

- Find out how PM is structured in **your** institution – follow this to the letter
- Be **transparent** throughout the process
- Avoid making judgements until all **evidence** is gathered and **discussion** is taking place
- Nurture the principle that you want all of your staff to be **successful** and **communicate** this
- **Enjoy** the process of helping colleagues to move themselves to the next level of professional performance

Sorting out problems with staff

You may sometimes need to help to resolve **disputes** and defuse **tensions** between people in your team. Teachers become excellent at doing this with youngsters in their charge and the principles are similar for adults.

1. Try to create a physical environment which is conducive to discussion
2. Focus on listening to the person and build rapport
3. Where there are strong emotions like anger and frustration, let the person vent them where possible
4. Once they have vented their emotions, ask them how they would prefer things to be
5. Ask them what the situation is currently like
6. Relay back to them what they said they wanted it to be like
7. Ask them what they think they need to do to achieve this and what help they need from others

This process maintains a sense of **empowerment** whilst still supporting the individual. Ignoring small issues usually results in more serious ones emerging later.

Competency

The issue of employment law is highly complex. In schools it is doubly so, given that two sets of laws govern schools. Firstly, there are Acts of Parliament and European directives and secondly, the specific education statutes enshrined in the now revised School Standards and Frameworks Act 1998. Sections 35 and 36 of this Act require that governors, local authorities and headteachers in schools pay attention to any subsequent Statutory Guidance issued by The Secretary of State for Education. Such guidance was issued in 2009 to bolster the 2002 Act. Schools have unique employment regulation with enhanced safeguarding procedures and heavy trade union involvement.

Where an employee cannot, or will not, act in accordance with the demands of their contract there may be reason to invoke capability proceedings. Your school will have its own policy on this. There will be expectations upon you as a line manager to support and keep records in connection with anyone at risk of capability proceedings. Always discuss this with your senior team and seek advice from them, your governors and LA. If you want to know more, Oliver Hyam's weighty tome *Employment in Schools: A Legal Guide* will provide you with more depth.

Delegating work

Most managers are unable to manage effectively unless they delegate work to others in their team. In many cases others can do things as well as you or better. It is important to the motivation and professional development of others that they have opportunities to carry out new tasks.

> *Delegation is not abcdication*

When you delegate you give **authority** to another to carry out a task on your behalf. They do not, however, have overall responsibility for the task – that stays with you. When you delegate you need to ensure:

- Adequate **authority** is given to the person so they can do the job. Colleagues need to know that you have authorised the person to act on your behalf
- They know exactly what their **responsibility** is, ie they have clear parameters for the task
- They know who they are **accountable** to
- They have the necessary **skills**, **resources** and **support**

Working with your second in department

Setting clear **boundaries of responsibility** for your second in department is the best way to ensure that work gets done.

Tips for working with your second in department:

- Recognise the **need** to delegate work in order to manage your department effectively, and your duty to train your second to do this work
- Review regularly the second in department's **role** and **responsibilities**
- Have regular **meetings** with them to discuss key issues
- Be ready to **listen** more than you speak
- Be aware of the **workload** that your second is carrying and take steps to manage this
- Carefully discuss **new areas** you are delegating to ensure that your second has a clear idea of what is **expected** and the appropriate level of **support** to achieve it
- Give balanced **feedback** along the way
- **Thank them** for the tasks they perform well
- **Don't** treat your second in department like an admin assistant. They need to learn the ropes for when they head up their own team

Continuing professional development

The professional head of department constantly looks to review their own skills and knowledge and to develop the skills and knowledge of others. Continuing professional development (CPD) is a crucial part of this process.

Engaging in CPD:

Broadens your outlook ✓

Keeps you **up to date** ✓

Encourages **flexibility** ✓

Prompts **questions** about existing practice ✓

Reminds you what can be **exciting** and what can be **demotivating** about learning ✓

The most effective CPD comes from internal motivators like the joy of learning, or a desire to improve pupil achievement, rather than from imposed training activities. Additionally, adult learning experiences where teachers are fully involved in learning communities and engaged in dialogue tend to be effective too (Dixon N. 2013). Add to that, learning which is absolutely central to the core purpose of the teacher's work and you have a winning formula.

Effective CPD Provision

The development of new teachers within your team is a great asset to the department; it also drives succession planning for the school and the profession as a whole. Research indicates that high quality CPD improves student learning (Thompson & Wiliam, 2008). For CPD to be at its most effective (according to Joyce & Showers 1996) it should involve a number of levels of support which combine to have a positive learning effect:

Coaching on the job — 5

Feedback on performance in simulated/real settings — 4

Practice in simulated settings — 3

Modelling of skills — 2

Presentation of approaches — 1

There is also compelling evidence to show that **coaching** by peers is a highly effective way to enable teachers to improve their practice. Coaching is a **core function** of the effective 21st Century head of department. There's more information about coaching and leadership at http://visionforlearning.co.uk, and for a guide to solution-focused coaching see the *Coaching & Reflecting Pocketbook*.

Identifying staff development needs

Having regular conversations with your team and your own line manager about developing yourself and your team is very important.

Using a coaching methodology for drawing out of others what their aspirations and desires are, allows you to match the growing needs of the department and the school with the natural interests and motivations of the people you lead.

Useful coaching questions include:

Where do you see yourself in 3 years? And what would you like to be doing then? What can we do here to support that? What opportunities would you like to develop your skills and capacities?

It's also important to find out what learning preferences they might have. The traditional CPD method of shadowing a colleague, going on a course or gathering in the school hall for an INSET session led by an outside expert can still be appropriate, but ICT, coaching, action research and blended approaches to learning are now possible.

Identifying appropriate CPD

Focus on ensuring that the CPD you arrange for your team matches their **needs** and is of the appropriate **quality**. There is a range of flexible approaches you could employ to suit budgets, learning styles and the challenges of time and location:

- Networking groups with other professionals and exam board work
- TeachMeets (http://teachmeet.pbworks.com)
- Webinars/webchats via Skype or other group chat platforms
- Online learning programmes
- Face-to-face INSET courses (The Good CPD Guide* is very helpful here)
- Shadowing others
- Trio/ one-to-one coaching
- Lesson Study trio planning and review*
- Books, journals and online video/podcast material

*See The Teacher Development Trust (http://tdtrust.org)

Remember: **choice** and **relevance** are big motivators for adult learning.

Maintaining resilience and managing stress

Everyone has an internal **resilience** bank account. When you continue to draw on your resilience bank account without putting anything back in, your account becomes **overdrawn**.

This overdraft leads to stress, reduced performance, damaged relationships and, eventually, ill health. Over a long period it can shorten your life.

There are inevitably times of unexpected demand in your role. These will draw on your reserves and can actually be exciting. However, if you have few reserves within you, then you will begin to experience all demands as negative **stress**.

Maintaining resilience and managing stress

How to **minimise** stress:

- Plan **ahead** – long, medium and short term, blocking out planning time each week and taking it (see pages 28-31)
- Be **realistic** with your plans and realistic in estimating the time tasks will take
- Be **flexible** towards your plans and build in enough margin for coping with unexpected demands – a head of department will always have them!
- Make **lists** and tick off things you achieve – praise yourself
- Take **time out** during the day – psychologically, even a few seconds without stimulus can be helpful
- Eat and drink **healthily**, especially water
- Create time for **exercise** and **mental space**
- Do something for **YOU** each week, something that you enjoy and look forward to
- Seek **help** from others if you feel you are suffering from too much stress, part of your role is to manage the workload and stress of the team – start with **YOU**!

How you manage **your** stress affects how you manage your **team's** stress

Recruiting and selecting staff

When you decide to recruit a new team member they may be in your team for the duration of your time in post. Choose wisely.

It is usual for headteachers to organise the advertisement process.

Before the interview:

- Make sure the **job specification** and **person specification** are sound and that those on the interview panel understand both
- Plan how you will **identify** whether the candidates have met the specification on paper and on the interview day
- **Shortlist** candidates from their paperwork by looking for evidence that they meet the person specification
- Invite as **many** people as you can manage to interview on the day, since candidates sometimes drop out on the morning of the interview
- Ensure they have all the **information** they will need for the interview, in good time

Recruiting and selecting staff

On the selection day:

As we interview the candidates, they interview us

- **Plan** carefully so your focus is on the recruitment process
- Give candidates a **tour** of the department and school, and sell the benefits (this is a good opportunity for them to meet staff and students)
- Observe them teaching a class

In the formal interview:

- Set candidates **at ease** – you'll get more information this way
- Be **consistent** with your core questions across the candidates
- **Balance** the kinds of questions asked – open and hypothetical questions can be most revealing
- Allow candidates the chance to **ask** questions – what they ask is an insight!
- Don't be afraid to explore **issues** which come up in the interview
- **Listen** to the views of the panel and make **your** views clear

Preparing for inspection

Inspections can often strike fear into heads of department, especially those who have not been through the experience before. However, if you are doing the right things throughout the year, inspection will not be an issue for you. With short-notice inspections the norm in most cases, preparing for inspection is about doing the right thing all of the time.

In recent years there have been a number of hasty revisions to the Ofsted process, and expectations have changed each time. Currently, being able to show student progress through data and students' work is fundamental to a successful inspection. This sits alongside observations of teaching and the consequent learning in classrooms. You cannot 'fudge this' for the inspection; it's part of your ongoing professional work to ensure that the right practices are in place even when the Ofsted eyes are not in the school.

The criteria for inspections are regularly revised, so make sure you refer to the latest information at www.ofsted.gov.uk

Preparing for inspection

Things to bear in mind in preparation for Ofsted:

Managing the department

- Carry out periodic audits or self-evaluations to identify your department's strengths and weaknesses

- Know your departmental data and the learners who are underperforming, and make sure your team knows it too

- Be able to explain confidently what you are doing about underperformance in students and staff

- **Support** your team through any anxieties about the process, and seek support yourself from a more senior member of staff if necessary

- Be ready to professionally and **assertively** make your case – you will sway even the most aggressive of Ofsted inspectors if you are confident and rational

- It is sensible to carry out a 'mock' Ofsted interview with a senior leader LA adviser, or private consultant – ask them to be the worst Ofsted inspector they have ever encountered!

Preparing for inspection

Things to bear in mind in preparation for Ofsted:

Teaching and learning

- **Observe** the teaching of all members of your department prior to the inspection, providing guidance and support as you do so
- Have **supportive**, **caring**, but **challenging** conversations throughout the year with colleagues to drive up performance
- Putting on **special lessons** for inspectors can unsettle students; making doubly sure everything is well organised will not
- Ofsted inspectors want to see the teachers in your department succeed in the classroom and enjoy their teaching – but their focus is on the **learning** that results from the teaching so always focus on **impact** of teaching
- Remind your team of your departmental **focus**: high quality teaching and learning that leads to excellent outcomes for learners

During the inspection

When the inspection is taking place:

- Be **confident**, and have faith in your own professional judgement – you are a great teacher and departmental manager!
- **Welcome** inspectors into your department as you would any visitor
- Try to keep things as normal as possible, focusing on **high quality** teaching and learning in your department
- Be there to **support** the members of your team but do not keep asking them if things are OK – your behaviour will set the tone for them
- Spend a few minutes at the end of day with your **team**, reviewing how the day went, discussing any lessons that were observed and sharing any concerns

The inspection interview

You may have a short interview with an inspector about progress, leadership and management issues in your department.

During your interview:

- Know your data and your strengths and weaknesses, but remember you are not here to please your inspector, you are presenting your **professional** case

- In answering their questions, get across your **philosophy** for effective teaching and learning

- Answer questions **professionally** and **confidently**. Even the most aggressive inspectors have been swayed by a rational and assertively presented argument

- Make the inspector aware how **long** you have been in post, what you have **done** so far and what your **plans** are for the future

- Be prepared to stand up for your own **professional judgement** about how you manage your department – there is no single 'right' way to do it and you know your school context better than the inspector

- Ensure that your **rationale** for leading your subject area is linked closely to the learner progress agenda

After the inspection

If you are pleased with the report on your department
Celebrate the fact that someone else has recognised your professionalism and hard work and that of your team, but remind yourself that you didn't need Ofsted to confirm you were doing a good job!

- Consider the suggestions for improvement with your team and form a realistic, written action plan
- Share the findings with your students – they will be curious to know what the inspectors thought of their school

If the report highlights weaknesses you feel powerless to address
- Try not to take things personally – easier said than done, but it's just a job remember!
- There is no failure only feedback – find a way to accept what cannot be changed and move into a mindset of dealing with the changeable factors
- Talk to your headteacher about the issues and what can be done to help
- Devise an action plan that involves the support of other people

If the report is unfair
- Make your headteacher aware of your concerns straight away so the inspection report can be challenged

Making the most of your budget

One of your key roles is to **manage your department's finances** effectively. Your headteacher will want to know that you are spending your budget wisely and in accordance with your departmental development/ improvement plan.

At all times keep in mind the aim of your departmental budget: **To ensure effective teaching and learning and progress for all students in your subject area**. Begin planning for the new year as soon as you can.

- Think again about your **departmental vision**
- R**eview** your departmental development/ improvement plan
- Be clear what the spending **priorities** are for the coming year
- Have computer **spreadsheets** ready to record spending in the new year
- **Shop around** to get the best value and order in **good time**

Many heads of department are now supplementing their budgets with external fundraising activities. See page 70 for further details. Check the appropriateness of any such activities with your headteacher, however.

Planning a budget

Plan your budget carefully to make sure finances are allocated appropriately. There are many different systems in operation in schools, so you must adapt yours to fit in with local circumstances. But areas which may need to be covered include:

- Text books
- Stationery
- ICT equipment
- Specialist equipment (and its service/repair) particular to your subject area
- Contributions to departmental trips

In many schools, exercise books and furniture are covered by a separate budget. Set yourself an upper limit for each spending heading, in line with what you can afford.

Running a budget

Liaise closely with your **school bursar** during the school year to keep track of your expenditure and any income from school trips or student purchases of books/equipment.

- Ask for a monthly **breakdown** for your department and **file** these statements carefully. Plan in a monthly review time to look at your budget
- Keep scrupulous **records**, preferably on computer spreadsheets
- Be aware of the **limits** that have been set under each spending heading
- Keep a particularly close eye on the **photocopying bill**
- Make sure your budget is **transparent** to the rest of your departmental team
- Have tight **systems** for collecting money from students for trips, books, etc
- Keep petty cash in a safe place

Selecting and protecting resources

Selecting resources

- **Shop around** to get best value – who could do this for you?
- Ask colleagues in other schools for **advice**
- Read **reviews** in subject magazines and online
- Ask for **trial** or **demonstration** models to try out different brands
- Request **approval** copies of books to make the best choice

Protecting resources

- Back all books with plastic coating
- Have a good system for **issuing** and **retrieving** books loaned out to students
- Put **school details** in books that are borrowed (otherwise they tend to walk off!)
- Mark larger or expensive items with **security codes**
- Adopt **protocols** for student use of equipment to minimise wear and tear
- Ensure that colleagues in your team understand the importance of **counting** resources out and back in during lessons
- Design **storage systems and areas** to make it easy to see when equipment or books are in use or missing

Raising additional income

There has been an upsurge in interest by schools in **external fundraising** in recent years. Many heads of department are finding fundraising activities a useful way to increase their budget. Such activities can also help develop innovative curriculum projects.

External funding sources include:

- National Lottery
- Charitable trusts
- Local businesses / business network groups
- European Union
- Competitions and awards
- School appeals and events, eg sponsored walk, table top sale

The website Grants 4 Schools (www.grantsalert.com) is an invaluable site to find out about the most appropriate funding sources.

Health and safety issues

You have a duty as a head of department to make sure that students being taught and the staff who work with them are **safe**, and that all reasonable steps have been taken to **minimise the risks** they might be exposed to. This includes time when they are off-site during school trips or educational visits linked to your subject area. The behaviour and safety of pupils is currently enshrined in the Ofsted framework for schools in England.

The nature of the risk depends very much on the subject being taught or on your particular school buildings and infrastructure. Nevertheless, many accidents in schools are not caused by especially hazardous equipment, eg:

- Fundamental safety issues posed by student and adult behaviour in school
- Trips and slips, including over cables and leads
- Students toppling off chairs
- Eye injuries caused by everyday classroom equipment

Having a well thought through **health and safety policy** for your department is an effective way to be proactive in managing the risk in your subject area.

Health and safety issues

An effective **health and safety policy** has the following characteristics:

- It makes clear that **health and safety awareness** is a key element of departmental practice
- It identifies the main **risks** and outlines the steps that have been taken to **minimise** these
- It emphasises the role **students and staff** can play in helping to minimise risk by responsible and thoughtful behaviour
- It explains the **procedures** that will be adopted if things go wrong

If you have concerns about the risks presented by a school building, or equipment in a poor state of repair, it is vital to alert your headteacher **straight away**.

Health and safety on school visits

Special care needs to be taken to ensure that all school visits are organised with **safety** in mind for both students and staff.

Schools must have a **designated member of staff** responsible for overseeing school visits, so that the procedures are adhered to. In particular, assessments must be carried out for all visits, where the risks are clearly identified along with measures to minimise them.

Governors and headteachers now must **approve** all such visits, and can refuse to let the trip go ahead if there are concerns about health and safety issues. This applies to seemingly low-risk activities such as theatre or museum visits, as well as outdoor activities and sports.

Health and safety on school visits

Good practice in organising school visits includes:

- **Planning** a long way ahead to allow the necessary forms to be filled in and clearances to be given by your headteacher/governors
- **Practising** filling in the risk assessment forms if you have not done this before
- **Liaising** with your school or LA visits co-ordinator if you have doubts about the activities to be undertaken
- Having an appropriate **student-adult ratio** in proportion to the activity to be undertaken, briefing staff carefully and ensuring safeguarding policy is adhered to in relation to adult supervision
- **Briefing parents/carers** about the health and safety procedures for the visit and informing them of any specific clothing/footwear or other items (eg sun cream) needed for the visit
- **Briefing students** before and on the day of the visit of the main risks and what they can do to stay safe

Remember (if appropriate) to consult **local authority guidance** on school visits and follow school safeguarding policy in setting up and protecting learners whilst on visits.

Effective Documentation

The departmental handbook

The departmental handbook is a guide to the **procedures** in your department and sets the tone for the **culture** you want to cultivate. Culture is defined as, 'the way we do things here'. Your handbook should cover:

- **Vision** – set out the future aspirations for the subject
- **Values** – communicate the shared values of the department within the school
- **Procedures and calendars** – outline every system and procedure specific to your department and a timetable of events and deadlines for the year
- **Collegiality** – show how everyone plays their part
- **Culture** – communicate the culture of the department within the context of the school

Aim for:

- **Currency** – it must be up to date
- **Accessibility** – it must be easily accessible to all those who need it
- **Word economy** – it must express the key principles and procedures in plain English (set a target for the number of pages and stick to it)

Policies and procedures

Departmental **policies** are an important basis for your work. They help to set the context and provide a common point of reference for all members of the department. They should meet the 'If I fell under a bus tomorrow' test, ie if you were suddenly indisposed could someone else pick up the handbook and carry on without you?

Top tips for writing effective policies:

- Tie them into the whole school policies – your department is not an island!
- Make them **simple** to understand
- Explain them in as **few words** as possible – 5-10 key points maximum
- Develop them with your **team**
- Consider **web-based or other e-format** policies for currency
- Build a quick reference **summary** into the document
- Don't be **precious** about them – they will change and need updating!

Schemes of work

There is an expectation that **schemes of work** be in place for every unit of work taught in your department. Schemes of work are produced from an overall curriculum map for each key stage, which ensures that concepts and ideas are progressively built with learners.

Key points about preparing schemes of work:

- Know how many **lessons** are available to devote to a scheme of work
- Decide level of detail required
- They are best produced by **multiple authors**, so decide a house style
- Have **standard** layout to promote consistency of content and process
- Be **inventive** where time is short, eg use homework well to creatively increase contact time

Lesson planning

Agree and adopt a departmental **lesson structure** that can be turned into an effective planning format. The one below is broadly adapted from US educational theorist, David Kolb.

Part 1: put the learning in context (about 5% of lesson time)

- Explore what the students learnt in the previous lesson
- Relate the learning to the overall syllabus
- Make the learning outcomes clear
- Explain what is coming in the next lesson
- Mind maps can be a very useful visual tool for this part of the lesson, showing students how an individual lesson fits into the wider course

Part 2: starter (about 10% of lesson time)

- Begin with a short activity which engages students' interest – a prop, story, exciting stimulus material
- Try to help students put what they already know about the topic in context
- Prepare the students for the main teaching and learning that will follow

Lesson planning

Part 3: main teaching and learning (about 75% of lesson time)

- Students should be carrying out activities for as much of this time as possible
- You should act as a facilitator for their learning – try not to talk for too long
- Students should be engaged in multi-sensory learning that respects their learning styles and intelligence profiles
- All students should be set work which is of an appropriate level of challenge
- Allow choice over how students carry out tasks
- Learning should be broken down into achievable chunks
- Find plenty of opportunities to develop thinking skills

Part 4: plenary (about 10% of lesson time)

- Provides an opportunity for learning to be reviewed
- Students should be given the chance to reflect on what they think the main learning points of the lesson have been

For an extensive set of ideas, resources and frameworks for teaching see Best & Thomas, (2007/8) *Creative Teaching and Learning Toolkit* and *Resource Books*

Effective planning

Here is a potential lesson plan tool which could be adapted as you see fit.

Programme of study or syllabus reference:	Module/topic title:	
Main learning objectives:		Lesson number: __ of __
Spiritual, moral, social and cultural values:	Putting the learning in context:	
Provision mapping considerations (SEN) lower/ middle/ higher attainment		
Key skill opportunities:	Starter activity:	
Literacy opportunities:	Main teaching and learning:	
Numeracy opportunities:	Details of teaching:	
	Details of learning activities:	
Assessment opportunities:	Plenary activity:	Homework tasks:

To an extent lesson planning can be a collaborative activity. However, individual lesson plans should take account of the needs of every child in a class or group.

The departmental improvement plan

The **improvement plan** (or development plan) is a document in which the school communicates its vision and targets for the future to itself and its stakeholders. Your department will need its own **development** or **improvement plan**.

It will be closely connected to the school's plan and the part your department plays in that. Be sure to address how the department will make its contribution to the whole school targets for the year. You may also have department-specific areas you wish to develop. These should also go into your plan.

Your work on vision and determining direction, (see page 14 onwards), remains a core part of creating your development plan. Your department is part of the whole institution and your department goals should flow from those of the whole.

Maximising
Student
Achievement

Developing a climate for effective learning

A climate for effective teaching and learning does not happen by accident – it has to be **cultivated** and steps taken to actively **maintain** it.

Cultivating the right environment

- Make **effective learning for all** your departmental focus
- Expect every student to try their best
- Be clear what you expect in terms of student behaviour and make it known that poor behaviour is not a feature of your department
- Reinforce what you want your students to learn
- Minimise learner stress

Maintaining a positive learning environment

- Celebrate achievement and effort
- Teach students how to learn and promote independent learning
- Encourage students to take risks in their learning
- Build effective relationships with students

Improving teaching and learning

Although you may already be proud of it, begin with the premise that teaching in your department, including your own, can be continually improved.

Active steps to improve teaching and learning include:

- Agreeing what constitutes **effective** teaching and learning in your subject area
- **Sharing** good practice, especially by watching each other teach
- Devoting departmental meeting time to **reflecting** on teaching and learning issues
- Using **self-evaluation** tools (see pages 110–125) to focus on specific aspects of teaching and learning
- Asking the **students** for their opinions
- Tackling staff underperformance **early**, in a caring but clear way, before issues build up

Accelerated learning

More and more teachers are discovering the benefits of so-called **accelerated learning** in their classrooms. Accelerated learning occurs when teachers take account of the way our brains like to learn, to design more effective learning experiences. It has been put on the educational map by inspirational trainers such as Alistair Smith.

Accelerated learning has enabled those departments committed to implementing a comprehensive programme of change to take advantage of the latest findings on the brain and learning. They have seen how to prepare students more effectively for learning, and how to design lessons with preferred learning styles and multiple intelligences in mind.

Gaining the benefits of accelerated learning:

- Go on an introductory course if the subject is new to you. There are many excellent ones available that provide a foundation for creating an accelerated learning department (see Further Information section)
- The *Accelerated Learning Pocketbook* (Best 2011) contains a **concise overview** of this exciting development in teaching and learning, together with a self-evaluation tool

Working with individual students

Encourage teachers in your department to gear their planning and work as much as possible towards the needs of **individual** students.

Promote work at the individual level by:

- Ensuring teachers talk to a few individuals in **detail** each lesson about their work
- Asking **open** questions about students' work
- Making sure that written and verbal feedback is appropriately **targeted**
- Helping students to take a real **interest** in their own progress, for example by a student record card of marks and achievement in your subject area
- Asking students to **talk** in detail about their own progress during student review evenings, using a pre-prepared prompt sheet to help them

Student target setting

Targets can help students make progress in line with – or hopefully above – expectations based on prior attainment. However, poorly thought-out target setting can damage student confidence. Grade targets below the magic thresholds are intensely demotivating for most learners. Here are some thoughts on setting great targets:

- Set **SMART** targets (specific, measurable, achievable, relevant, time-related)
- **Involve students** in the setting of their own targets
- **Break targets down** into smaller ones using Olympic Goal-setting
    - My long term goal is: (eg get a job in recruitment; therefore I need... ...)
    - Interim targets are: (eg by Christmas I am getting ... ... By February I am able to... ...)
    - Behavioural goals are: (eg in order to achieve these goals I need to be completing homeworks regularly, asking for help when I'm stuck ... ...)
- Include targets for **effort and skill acquisition** as well as attainment, particularly for students who struggle to achieve academically

Consistency across the department

Your department will be more effective if you strive for **consistency** in setting, marking and assessing work, and reporting on students' performance. This can be achieved by:

- Sampling students' **exercise books** to ensure standards of marking are consistent across all teachers
- Ensuring the marking is **moderated** wherever internal test data is used for setting or examination tiering
- Preparing exemplar material so that expected standards are made clear to all teachers
- Marking work **collectively** from time to time to discuss the process, compare outcomes, and define the marking expectations
- Writing **mark schemes** collaboratively
- **Cross-moderating** each other's marking
- Ensuring all teachers use the same system for **report** writing, and that judgements are made consistently

Working with parents/carers

Parents and carers should be **partners** in the learning of the students you teach. Be aware of sensitivities that may exist where parents/ carers are in dispute with one another but, broadly speaking, **involve** them in their children's learning by:

- Spending **quality time** with them on student review evenings – this should be at least five minutes in duration, uninterrupted and focused on the student's progress
- Inviting them to **come into school** at other times for further discussions or to observe lessons if this is appropriate in your school
- Asking them to make **comments** in their child's homework diary about work in your subject area
- **Suggesting** things they can do to help their child make better progress

Parents and carers represent the hugely **diverse communities** of 21st Century life. Ensure you are inclusive, open and non-judgmental in dealing with them.

Dealing with attainment data

There is a wealth of **data** on students' performance now available. Indeed, sometimes schools seem to be suffering from data overload, with hundreds of different types of data routinely being gathered and many kinds published for public scrutiny.

There is no doubt that there are some rich **data sources** that can be used to help a head of department understand the patterns of achievement in their subject area. Data can help set student achievement targets for the department and monitor how well individual students are progressing. The types of data available include:

- National test results
- CAT scores
- Teacher assessments
- Mid-YIS, YELLIS and ALIS tests
- GCSE, diplomas and A-level results
- Internal test data
- Value-added data

How is attainment data useful?

You can use attainment data in a **variety** of ways, including:

- Charting the progress of **individual** students
- Setting realistic end of course/ exam **targets** for groups or individuals based on prior attainment – but make sure they are negotiated with the students
- Picking out any **patterns of underachievement** for groups of students eg the vulnerable
- Discovering **gaps** in students' knowledge that need to be filled
- Identifying areas of **good practice** to be celebrated and shared
- Determining areas of the curriculum that need to be **taught** differently according to learner needs
- Identifying **gifted and talented** students

Your school will have software and data experts to consult. Use this expertise to help you. Other data can also be very helpful such as attendance, pupil feedback surveys, and behaviour logs. Data raises useful questions and shows patterns; it's something to become familiar with and to use to spot inconsistencies and potential problems.

Inclusion

There are few things more important than making sure every student in your care makes good progress and is not held back due to any specific barriers to learning, or individual needs. If you get this right, then you have a truly **inclusive** department.

At the time of going to press the English guidelines on inclusion and meeting the special needs of learners in schools, are in a state of flux. The advent of Provision Mapping, and changes in the funding and support for SEN are unlikely, however, to change the principles of inclusivity and equal opportunity for children in the UK.

Excellent provision is about adopting a **mindset** where every student is treated as an individual, with particular strengths, weaknesses and needs. These may be based on their educational needs or on other aspects of their social, moral, spiritual, and diversity requirements.

What you do in the classroom to help individuals make progress can make a radical difference to whether a student is successful at school and goes on to live a fulfilled life. Inclusion really is that important to the long term success of children.

Creating an inclusive department

Steps to making your department more inclusive

1. Have a **vision** of what your inclusive department would look like.
2. Identify the **specific barriers** to learning of individual students, or those with particular **needs** (eg gifted & talented, cultural diversity, sexual orientation and gender, social issues, psychological conditions, specific learning difficulties).
3. Challenge beliefs that undermine inclusivity in learners, parents/ carers and staff.
4. Implement **measures** to help students overcome barriers to learning or progress better.
5. Utilise **teaching assistants** or **support assistants** where appropriate.
6. Track the **progress** of individuals and groups.
7. **Celebrate** your efforts to create an inclusive department.

Inclusive departments tend to feature in schools with an inclusive ethos – your headteacher has a lead role in this respect.

Supporting students' learning

Coaching students can be a very effective way to help them make progress.

In getting the best from your students you need to encourage them to think for themselves. The key to this is to get them to set their own goals to solve problems and plan their learning. The STRIDE model of coaching provided on page 38 can be used here too. The following questions can help them do this:

1. What do you want to achieve? (be really specific)
2. How will you know when you have achieved it?
3. What is the situation at the moment?
4. What have you tried so far?
5. What stands in the way of you achieving this goal?
6. What if this thing were not there? What would you do then?
7. What will move you one step further forward to achieving this vision?
8. When will you do it?

The questions may be varied and can be spoken or displayed where students can use them on their own. Students might like to formulate their own questions.

Removing barriers to learning

Coaching students beyond the stage where they are stuck can be as simple as asking the right **questions**.

When students get stuck:

1. Get them to **define** exactly what they are trying to achieve (the goal)
2. Follow the questions on the previous page up to number six
3. Then when they say what is holding them back (X), ask **incisive questions**
   What would you do if X was not there?
   What would you do if you didn't have to live with the consequences?
   Who do you admire? How would they tackle this and get the result you want?

These questions suspend the **limiting beliefs** that can hold students back and they generate new solutions. Finish by asking them what they will do and when.

These and other specialised support techniques can be **learned**. Visit www.visionforlearning.co.uk for details of coaching courses for teachers.

Working with higher attaining students

The government continues to place emphasis on the needs of the most able students, who have been termed 'gifted and talented'. As a result, Ofsted inspections may well look specifically at this pupil group.

Schools have been encouraged to identify a cohort of each year group as 'gifted and talented' (typically 5 – 10%), with the 'talent' category referring to ability in art, performing arts or sport.

Good departmental practice in working with more able students includes:

- Recognising the **characteristics** of the most able students in your subject area
- Asking each teacher to **identify** these students on a regular basis
- Keeping a **list** of those who have been identified
- Designing lessons that **challenge** and **inspire** these students
- Tracking their **progress**
- Asking the students for their views on how their learning could be aided
- Frequently asking yourselves the question *'Who are our most able students and how are we catering for them?'*

Managing challenging student behaviour

A lot of a head of department's time can be taken up dealing with **behaviour problems**, so it is important to be proactive in managing student behaviour. Achieving success with behaviour management owes much to cultivating a climate where poor behaviour simply 'does not happen' in your department.

Strategies for promoting positive behaviour

- Set up a clear **system** for managing behaviour in your department
- Have clear and consistent **expectations** about what constitutes positive behaviour
- Encourage students to get involved in setting **their own** class rules for positive behaviour
- Make time for students to talk about **feelings** and **attitudes**
- **Praise** positive behaviour
- Use **sanctions** sparingly but consistently and in line with a published policy
- Seek the **intervention** of a more senior member of staff if a situation becomes really serious

The ownership of behaviour

As head of department, you may be called upon to support a situation where a teacher is finding it difficult to manage a student or class. In these cases:

- Be clear about **school procedures** for dealing with challenging behaviour
- Always maintain the teacher's **authority** by working with them to support them and advise on managing the student's behaviour
- Avoid strategies wherever possible which involve **you** taking responsibility for the students' behaviour – this can undermine the position of the teacher
- Find out what has **already** been tried and what they have yet to try
- **Empathise** with the teacher and then support them to design the next step and take it – improving behaviour can take time
- Teachers sometimes escalate situations through their own behavior. Part of your **professional duty** (with a caring attitude) is to coach them towards better management of situations
- Try to find out what **triggers** the students' poor behaviour, offering to observe a lesson to help do this, especially if the teacher finds the triggers hard to identify
- Most importantly, **talk to the student** about the reasons for their behaviour – once their behaviour is understood all concerned can support the student to change it

The ownership of behaviour

Where the main approaches to behaviour management are unsuccessful you can consider other strategies:

- **Parent/ carer** involvement
- Individual or class **reporting** systems – with your support and with clear outcomes for success
- Temporary **removal** of a student from a classroom (they must always be given alternative support)
- Placing a student in an **alternative** group more appropriate for their needs

Remember: Focus on the **behaviour** not the person. The student may have self-esteem issues which have an impact on their behaviour. It is always better to have the normal class teacher deal with the situation (with your support), before escalating the intervention. Educating the student in their normal classroom is always the best solution.

Sustainable behaviour management

Sustainable behaviour management is largely about **prevention** rather than cure. Researchers consistently show that **rewards** work more effectively than **sanctions**.

Some **proactive** approaches to managing behaviour:

- Make lessons **exciting, engaging** and **appealing** to a range of learning styles and intelligences
- **Involve** students in setting or re-setting classroom rules – and display them prominently
- Ensure that students have the opportunity for structured **input** into discussions and decisions made in the classroom
- Ensure that students have a clear understanding of the **purpose** of the work they are doing and that it is set at an appropriate level of challenge
- Ensure the environment is **appropriate** for the kind of activity they are engaged in
- Develop systems of **reward** in line with school policy and **praise** students frequently. Avoid giving routine rewards for the same thing, as the students will come to value the reward not the learning achieved

Enriching learning

Find ways to **enrich** the curriculum for the students in your department, providing a break from traditional classroom learning.

Such enrichment opportunities could include:

- A whole day **cross-curricular** event or celebration – these can sometimes be linked up with national initiatives, such as Red Nose Day
- An educational **visit** (theatre, field trip)
- A **guest speaker/performer** – students really appreciate a break from their normal class teacher!
- Links with **industry**
  - Students involved in solving a real problem for a company
  - Industry/other outside agency delivering part of the curriculum in school or off site
- **Online** communication with experts

Raising the Profile of Your Department

Promoting your department

Many heads of department are recognising the need to **promote** their departments. When promoting your subject and department consider the following:

- What are the **benefits** of my subject to learners?
- What are the strengths of the **team** I have?
- What are the strengths of the **resources** I have?
- What are the strengths of the **students** we have?
- What do we **do** as a department that goes the extra mile?
- What have we got to be **proud** of?
- What **obstacles** have we overcome or are we managing well?

In any promotional work, focus on the strengths of your department. Always **talk up** your department. Remind colleagues of the importance of this in front of other colleagues, parents/carers and students.

Events

Events can be a great way of raising your profile and adding to learning.

Consider:
- Tying school events in with major **national** and **international** events
- Putting the department on the map with an unusual **challenge**
- Linking events to the school **newsletter** eg a monthly competition
- Asking **students** what they would like to organise

When organising events like this:
- Look for **support** from colleagues and delegate to them
- **Plan** carefully – a well-organised event will improve your departmental image
- **Advertise** well in advance – a well attended event is a successful one
- Consider the event from the students' point of view – what's in it for them?
- Think creatively about **funding** – who might add funding to your project?

Allow ample time for **planning** – there is such a thing as bad publicity!

Displays

Effective use of **displays** can really enhance the learning environment, but is often neglected in secondary schools.

What makes a display effective:

- **Ownership** – staff and students should play a part in creating it
- **Currency** – it should change regularly and be associated with current topic material
- **Colour** – it should be attractive and dynamic
- **Presentation** – it should be well put together, using good quality materials
- **Imagination** – bold simple ideas which communicate a message work well, eg 'photosynthesis makes sugars for green plants', or 'glacial valleys are U-shaped and river valleys are V-shaped'

Don't forget also the message the state of **décor** and **furnishings** in your department can give. Take steps to improve these so they provide an attractive background canvas for your students' work.

Working with the media

Using the **media** is a great way of promoting your successes. Handled well it can really propel your subject into the limelight. However, do consult your **senior management team** before inviting, or participating in, media coverage, and where students are involved, check the requirements regarding parental permission.

Some considerations:

- Be sure what **message** you want to convey
- With newspapers it is best to write your own **press release** and send it to the reporter – you are more likely to get your message right
- **Nurture** your relationships with journalists – they will serve you well
- **Don't pester** editors about your press releases – if you sent it they got it!
- With **radio** and particularly **television**, be really clear what kind of programme is being made before you agree to any recording – especially if they approach you first; it can be very time consuming to get involved in this kind of promotion work
- Make use of your school website and the potential of social media such as Twitter to promote your department's work

Making external links

Consider forging **links** with the community and outside agencies including the following:

- Local businesses
- Feeder schools
- Sixth form colleges
- University departments
- Teaching associations

There are a number of issues to consider in setting up these links, summarised in this **Relationship Cross Model**

OWNERSHIP
In the school and in the outside agency: who will manage the links overall and liaise with the outside partners? What is the role of the staff and students in building the relationships?

RESOURCES
What resources will be required and who will fund/provide them?

THE EFFECTIVE RELATIONSHIP

PURPOSE
What will be the purpose for you and the purpose and benefits to the outside agency?

CONTINUITY
How will the link be organised in purpose, time and space? How will you communicate in short, medium and long term?

Self-evaluation

Self-evaluation framework

To take a closer, more analytical look at your departmental practice:

1. Read the questions and **score** yourself by ticking the appropriate box
    0 = you feel you have not begun to address the question
    1 = you have started work, but it is in its early stages
    2 = you feel quite confident about the work you have done in this area
    3 = you feel the work you have done in this area represents excellent practice

2. As you do so note down any **action points** or issues that come to mind – this can form the basis of your action plan for improving your department.

3. Then **add up** the scores for each section and for the self-evaluation as whole. This will give you a **quantitative** assessment of the areas you need to develop.

4. Take a **photocopy** so you can refer back to it. You can repeat the exercise in six or twelve months' to judge your progress. In this way you should be able to identify the steps you need to take to become a more **advanced** departmental manager.

5. Formulate your action plan for improving your department, including who can help you make positive changes, and the timescale for the work.

Consider sharing the outcome of this evaluation with other members of your team and your senior management team mentor. Its quantitative nature allows you to draw charts and graphs that will assist others in making sense of the scores.

Self-evaluation framework

Vision, planning and goals	◁ Emerging		Advanced ▷	
	0	1	2	3
Do you have a clear departmental vision for the next five years?				
How effectively do you communicate your vision to others?				
To what extent is your vision shared by all members of the team?				
Are there strong links between your departmental vision and the whole school targets?				
Do you use a common framework for lesson planning across the department?				
Do you include health and safety issues as a key part of all planning?				
Do you set goals effectively using a goal-setting framework?				
Are you clear what your goals are for this week?				
Are you clear what your goals are for this year?				

Self-evaluation framework

Vision, planning and goals	◁ Emerging		Advanced ▷	
	0	1	2	3
Are you clear what your goals are for the next five years?				
Do you review departmental goals regularly and encourage others to do so?				
Do you make time each week to focus on progress towards long term goals?				
Do you book out time regularly to plan?				
Do you allow time each half-term to consider 'blue-sky' thinking in your department?				
Is the ownership of targets/goals amongst colleagues encouraged in your department?				

Vision, planning and goals score: ☐ /45 = ☐ %

Self-evaluation framework

Improving day-to-day management	Emerging 0	1	Advanced 2	3
Are you clear what your departmental strengths and weaknesses are?				
Are you aware of what needs to happen to improve your department?				
Do you understand the balance needed between leadership and management?				
To what extent is CPD encouraged in your department and for yourself?				
Do you make good use of your team's CPD experience?				
To what extent do you model the CPRS approach (see page 18)?				
Do you use a range of problem-solving strategies, including creative approaches?				
To what extent do you hold the belief that there is always a solution to a problem and that you will find it?				
To what extent do you proactively manage team spirit?				
Do you take measures to develop good rapport in your department?				

Self-evaluation framework

Improving day-to-day management	<Emerging 0	1	Advanced > 2	3
Do you make use of coaching and mentoring strategies?				
Is your feedback to staff constructive and developmental?				
To what extent do you manage meetings effectively?				
Is there a common structure for setting, marking and assessing students' work in your department?				
Is the reporting of students' achievements consistent across your department?				
Do you handle staff problems sensitively and supportively?				
Do you pay attention to authority, responsibility, accountability and support when delegating work?				
Is delegation used as a tool to help you manage the department more effectively?				
Do you use open-ended questions to promote independent decision-making among your team?				
Do you make time to listen to the successes and frustrations of your team?				

Self-evaluation framework

Improving day-to-day management	Emerging 0	1	Advanced 2	3
To what extent do you take steps to actively manage your own stress?				
To what extent do you take steps to actively manage your team's stress?				
Do you select new staff with care to ensure they will enhance the profile of your department?				
Do you enter negotiations with a plan for dealing effectively with the situation?				

Improving day-to-day management score: /72 = %

Self-evaluation framework

Managing finances	Emerging 0	1	Advanced 2	3
To what extent is your departmental spending focused on improving teaching and learning?				
Do you plan departmental spending as much in advance as is feasible in your school?				
Is your departmental spending linked to your departmental goals?				
Do you have effective systems in place for monitoring income and expenditure?				
To what extent are your departmental finances open to others in your team to encourage ownership of responsibility?				
Do you ensure best value when purchasing goods and services?				
Are there established departmental protocols in place to minimise the loss of resources through damage and pilfering?				
Do you try to raise additional income for your department from external sources?				

Managing finances score: /24 = %

Self-evaluation framework

Managing Ofsted or other inspection regime	Emerging 0	1	Advanced 2	3
Is Ofsted borne in mind in all of your planning to avoid last minute panic?				
Do you treat Ofsted inspections as a development tool for the department?				
Do you use periodic departmental audits to identify strengths and weaknesses before Ofsted inspectors arrive?				
To what extent do you feel able to justify your departmental policy/practice to your inspector?				

Managing Ofsted score: ☐ /12 = ☐ %

Self-evaluation framework

Effective documentation	Emerging 0	1	Advanced 2	3
Do you have an up to date departmental handbook?				
Do you have an up to date departmental development plan?				
Are subject policies on key issues in place?				
Are your subject policies revised in the light of recent developments?				
Are there schemes of work in place for all units of work?				
Are your schemes of work updated periodically to take account of new developments?				

Effective documentation score: ☐ /18 = ☐ %

Self-evaluation framework

Improving teaching and learning	Emerging 0	1	Advanced 2	3
Is high quality teaching and learning your department focus?				
Do you have an action plan for improving teaching and learning?				
Do you take steps to develop a positive climate for learning?				
Are you using accelerated learning principles?				
How focused is your department on independent learning?				
Do you observe the lessons of all teachers in your department on a rolling cycle?				
Do you carry out regular moderation of internal and external assessment work?				
Is lesson observation used to improve teaching and learning?				
Do all teachers ask students how they can improve their teaching and learning?				
Do you enrich the curriculum in your department through guest speakers, educational visits and other activities?				

Improving teaching and learning score: ⬚ /30 = ⬚ %

Self-evaluation framework

Working with individual students	Emerging 0	1	Advanced 2	3
Do all teachers in your department tailor their teaching as much as possible to the needs of individuals?				
Do you encourage students to formulate their own targets/goals?				
Are open questions used to help students find out what their needs are?				
Do you use coaching and mentoring techniques to support students' learning by helping them overcome barriers to success?				
Do all teachers in your department listen carefully to what students have to say about their learning?				
Is time taken at meetings to discuss and practise the communication skills which foster good relationships with individuals?				
Do you encourage students to monitor their own performance, for example via a record card?				

Working with individual students score: ☐/21 = ☐%

Self-evaluation framework

Promoting positive behaviour	◁ Emerging		Advanced ▷	
	0	1	2	3
Do you have high expectations of students regarding behaviour?				
Do you agree rules for classroom behaviour with students?				
Do you have a clear strategy for promoting positive behaviour?				
To what extent does your team separate the student from their behaviour when dealing with behavioural issues?				
Are practical approaches to managing student behaviour discussed in meetings?				
Do you make long-term plans and keep records for managing student behaviour?				
Do you periodically review the quality of teaching and learning opportunities and their impact on behaviour?				
Do you support colleagues in managing challenging behaviour without undermining their authority?				

Promoting positive behaviour score: /24 = %

Self-evaluation framework

Using student performance data	Emerging		Advanced	
	0	1	2	3
Do you share student performance data with colleagues?				
Do you explain the sources and uses of data to your team?				
Do you use a wide variety of data systematically to monitor the success of your department?				
Is data used proactively to identify possible areas for departmental development?				
Do you use data to pose questions about student and colleague performance?				
Is data used to set baselines for colleague and student performance?				
Do you consider how you might further enhance the use of data to better target resources and training?				
Do you analyse data to monitor the achievement of vulnerable groups of students?				

Using student performance data score: ☐ /24 = ☐ %

Self-evaluation framework

Promoting your department	◁ Emerging		Advanced ▷	
	0	1	2	3
Do you have a plan for promoting your department?				
Are you clear what departmental strengths you'd like to promote?				
Do you actively promote the achievements of your department within the school and with the press?				
Are students encouraged to take part in extra-curricular events organised by your department?				
Is display used to celebrate student achievement?				
Do you link display to current learning outcomes?				
Do you seek regular coverage for your department in the school newsletter/magazine?				
Do you encourage entry to local and national subject-related competitions?				
Do you seek external links for your department?				

Promoting your department score: ☐ /27 = ☐ %

Self-evaluation framework

Working with parents / carers	◁ Emerging		Advanced ▷	
	0	1	2	3
Do you have a plan for working more effectively with parents/carers?				
Are parents/carers seen as key partners in the education of the students in your department?				
Do you involve parents/carers closely when managing the behaviour of individual students?				
Do your students attend their review meetings with parents/carers?				
Do your students do much of the talking about their progress at the review meetings?				
Do you explain to parents/carers how they can create a positive learning environment at home?				
Do you encourage parents/carers to write comments in your students' homework diaries?				

Working with parents/carers score: ☐ /21 = ☐ %

Self-evaluation framework

Managing inclusion	Emerging 0	1	Advanced 2	3
To what extent are you a fully inclusive department?				
Do you have a plan to make your department more inclusive?				
Is there a departmental inclusion policy in place?				
Do you work tirelessly to reduce barriers to learning?				
Do you identify gifted and talented students?				
Are all learning activities differentiated for all levels of ability and learning styles?				

Managing inclusion score: ☐ /18 = ☐ %

KEY	
0-29%	emerging department
30-59%	established department
60-89%	advanced department
90%+	cutting edge department

TOTAL SCORE: ☐ /336 = ☐ %

Date evaluation was carried out: ☐ / /

Websites and books

www.brinbest.com Training, consultancy and publications for school leaders and teachers.

http://visionforlearning.co.uk Free resources and courses in coaching, NLP, leadership, managing workload and personal effectiveness.

Accelerated Learning Pocketbook
by B.J. Best. Teachers' Pocketbooks, 2011

Behaviour Management Pocketbook
by P. Hook & A. Vass. Teachers' Pocketbooks, 2011

Challenging Behaviour
by A. Copley. NEP (nee Bloomsbury) 2006

Coaching & Reflecting Pocketbook
by P. Hook, I. McPhail & A. Vass. Teachers' Pocketbooks, 2006

Coaching Solutions. Practical Ways to Improve Performance in Education
by W. Thomas & A. Smith. Continuum,

Coaching Solutions Resource Book
by W. Thomas. Network Educational Press, 2005

The Creative Teaching and Learning Toolkit and *Resource Books*
by B. Best & W. Thomas. Continuum 2007, 2008

Managing Workload Pocketbook
by W. Thomas. Teachers' Pocketbooks, 2005

The Mind Map Book
by T. Buzan & B. Buzan. BBC Books, 2000

Acknowledgements

Brin Best

I am grateful to all the staff at Settle High School & Community College for their professionalism and good humour. In particular Bob Hordern who was an excellent role model in my early years as an aspiring head of department, and Kathryn Needham with whom I began building a successful department. The self-evaluation framework in this book benefited from my work as part of the Inclusion Team at Barnsley LA, and I thank Elaine Doxey and Niki Elliot in particular for helping me understand more fully the issues surrounding inclusion. Finally, I place on record my heartfelt thanks to my wife Amanda and my parents for unfailing support and a healthy dose of realism when the going got tough.

Will Thomas

I would like to thank staff and students at South Bromsgrove Community College for their ongoing inspiration through their outstanding practice. I'm indebted to Mike Parry for his leadership and courage. I would also like to thank Phil McTague for his shining example of outstanding leadership. Grateful thanks go to Steve Clark for his superb advice and contribution on using data in this book. Thank you Neil Dixon for your excellent contributions to the CPD pages in this book. Thank you to the middle leaders of the Oaks Collegiate for their invaluable support with this edition. I dedicate this book to James Sterio: your love, light, courage, humour and enthusiasm are beyond measure.

Linda Edge has continued to be a wonderful support to this book. Thank you.

About the authors

Brin Best BSc (Hons), PGCE, FRGS, FMA, managed an award-winning geography department at Settle High School & Community College, prior to joining the advisory staff at the Barnsley School Effectiveness Team. He is now an education consultant specialising in school improvement and classroom innovation. Brin has a keen interest in effective teaching and learning strategies and has carried out research into thinking skills at Leeds University. He speaks widely on education issues, is the author of over 20 books and can be contacted via his website at www.brinbest.com.

Will Thomas BSc (Hons), MA, PGCE, led a highly successful science faculty at South Bromsgrove Community College. He has acted as an LA Advisor and prior to his teaching career was a personnel manager with Marks and Spencer. He is a qualified professional coach and therapist and runs Vision for Learning, a training and personal development company, providing coaching and training to schools and individuals. He is an award-winning and best-selling author of 14 books on coaching, leadership and creativity. Will can be contacted on +44 (0)1684 578754 or by email: info@visionforlearning.co.uk or through his website: www.visionforlearning.co.uk